D.A.Weaver

1

INTRODUCTION

One of the main reasons that many anglers have an unsuccessful fishing trip is down, not to the fish being somewhere else, but more down to missed bites and striking to soon.

The main objective of this book is to look at three main fishing types and how learning to master one, leads to more success in another, the main fish in this book are all members of the flat fish variety, however the methods used will ultimately help in catching other fish species not mentioned.

This book covers fishing from the rocks, beach, estuary and the boat where all the methods and techniques can literally be put together and result in the angler having a whole new experience in fishing.

The first and one of the most important things you need to do is to find a rod that you are comfortable with holding as with most types of fishing it is always best to hold the rod whilst you wait for a bite, you stand more than a 60% chance of catching and landing the fish if you are holding the rod when the fish bites, a rod rest is best used for setting up your rod or holding the rod while you have a tea or coffee etc. unless you just happen to be on a beach, there is a good place to use a rest for a number of reasons.

One of the other aims is to get the angler to take less tackle and equipment out on a fishing trip, there are a number of reasons for this, however the main ones are that if you are rock fishing then nine out of ten times you will not use most things i.e. a rod rest, seat box etc. also the more things you take with you, means the more you have to carry back over the rocks particularly after catching the species of fish you have gone after, so there you go, it makes sense.

BE SAFE, BE COMFORTABLE

Never fish alone, even a sprained ankle on the rocks, will probably need assistance, even a minor problem can become an emergency if you are alone. You should remember that in risking your own safety, you may also be risking the safety, or life of the members of the rescue services. Should you witness a serious problem, or be involved in an accident and can reach a telephone, you should dial 999 and ask for the Coast Guard. It is best when planning a fishing trip to let someone know where you are going and an approximate time that you expect to return.

In an emergency a Mobile phone can be of assistance, but remember that at sea level, and below cliffs, a signal may be weak or even non existent. Know where you are, this sounds obvious, but you must be able to direct assistance to where it is needed, if a swift response is required to an emergency.

Obtain a current Tide Table for the area, this will not only allow you to plan the times for your trip, but will also give you the approximate range of the tide so that you will not be cut off by rising water. Keep an eye on the state of the sea at all times.

A storm far out to sea can generate a swell which builds in height as it approaches land, this can quite easily flood over an apparently safe fishing platform. Some anglers use ropes to reach, and, or, secure themselves to a fishing platform, it is recommended that if a rope is needed for any of these, don't go! Approach the fishing mark by land, if you can walk or scramble down to the mark, then you can also expect to get off this mark safely.

When you approach a fishing mark from sea level at low tide you must either be certain of a dry route away, in the event of being cut off by the incoming tide, or you will have to be prepared to remain until the water level drops sufficiently, for you to return home safely, this can and often take approximately 6 hours.

There is a considerable link between being safe and the type of clothing we wear when fishing. Good strong footwear with soles that will resist slipping on wet rock, and with good ankle support, is the best type of footwear to use whilst fishing from the rocks. Ironically most of the best fishing marks require quite a lot of walking, often over rough terrain.

To partner the footwear, use a good pair of thick socks, in summer you will sweat less and in winter be warm. Even when beach fishing during the summer it is best not to go barefoot, a Weever fish sting or Razor shell cut can mar the trip and cause considerable pain.

During the summer months thin airy clothing is required, but you can still be cool and safe by wearing a floatation waistcoat, this modern floatation aid is light, comfortable, and does not impede your movement whilst fishing or casting.

A word of caution however, most of these floatation jackets and suits will give you adequate buoyancy should you fall in to the water, but they will not turn you face up in the way that a self righting inflatable jacket will. In winter a full flotation suit is ideal to give you an added safety advantage, in addition, coupled with several layers of thin clothing or a fleece one piece suit, will keep you warm on a frosty night.

Keep your head warm with a thick woollen hat or balaclava, and wear a thick pair, of neoprene gloves to keep the cold from your hands, during the winter you can spend more time trying to keep your hands warm than actual fishing.If buying new clothing for the purpose of fishing, get colours that are highly visible, military type combat clothing is designed for camouflage, these will keep you warm, however in the event of an accident, the visibility of clothing can play a major part in any rescue attempt.

When night fishing ensure that you have adequate lighting, either the liquid fuel anchor type lamp or a battery operated head lamp, to be sure that you have the correct light for the job at hand, you can always take both of these light sources with you. Many accidents can, and have occurred during the process of landing a fish. A heavy fish off the rocks, can tempt your companion to climb down to the waters edge for the purpose of hand lining the fish back up the rocks.

Use a landing net with a long handle or a long handled gaff (particularly for Conger eels). A drop net is the best solution from harbour walls, and piers.

You must however, make sure that you are on firm ground, and never over stretch your self or lean over the edge of where ever you are fishing, many falls are caused by people over stretching themselves.

below centre are a few things that the angler should take, particularly on night fishing trips, left is the winter wear, full floatation suit, suitable gloves and boots, right is the spring/summer wear, floatation waistcoat and suitable footwear, note both pictures have a woolly hat, one of the main things in winter is to keep your head warm and in summer it will also keep you cool whilst keeping the sun off your head.

FISH IDENTIFICATION

The fish shown in this book have one thing in common with each other, they are all flatfish and are the main ones caught from the boat and shores around the United Kingdom. Some of these fish are more plentiful than others, and many of these tend to look similar in size, shape, colour and with all having the same fin arrangement. The habitat in which fish live, swim and feed can greatly affect the colour and markings on different species of fish, these are no exception to the rule.

On many fish there may be a size limit in force, depending on which area of the U.K. you happen to be fishing, an example of this is the N.F.S.A, which work on a minimum size of the fish and the C.F.S.A. that work on the minimum weight.

if you are ever in doubt as to the limits on any species of fish, the best thing to do is to ask a local tackle dealer as he or she should be very willing to help, and should be up to date on the different limits in their area.

The M.A.F.F. can impose heavy fines if an angler is caught with under size fish. If whilst fishing you happen to get stung, cut or bitten by any fish, it is wise to seek medical advice, some fish in the waters around the United Kingdom can be venomous or have sharp spines, which can cause infection.

Under sized fish that are to be returned to the sea should be handled carefully, it is best to handle them with wet hands or a damp towel, as this will prevent causing any damage to the fish scales, fins, eyes and rest of body.

If returning a fish to the sea it is best to carry it down to the waters edge and not drop it from a great height, but also remember, safety first, do not risk your or anyone else's life for a fish, it's just not worth the risk!

FISH IDENTIFICATION DIAGRAM

The diagram provided is for the angler to examine so that he or she should be able to determine the correct name of fins etc. and in doing so help towards the identification of various species and individual fish, however if in doubt, check with your local tackle dealer, he or she should be able to help with any identifying marks that may have been missed by the angler.

Another problem may also arise when certain flatfish are caught as some members of flatfish interbreed, common examples are the flounder and plaice, however these cross breeds tend to be put in with the flounder species as when this occurs the flounder tend to be the dominant fish.

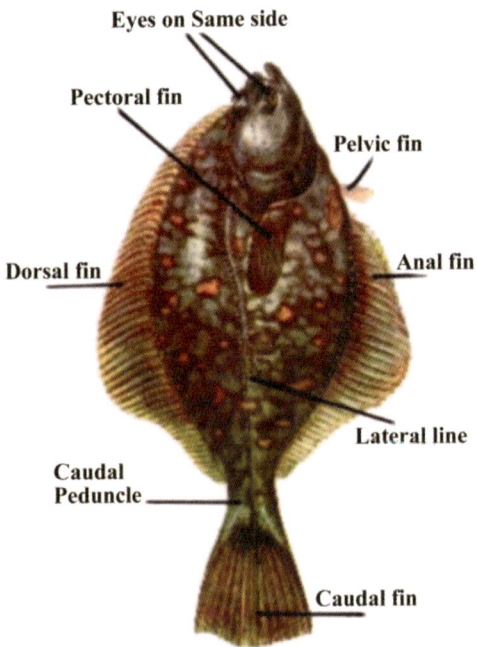

Eyes on Same side
Pectoral fin
Pelvic fin
Dorsal fin
Anal fin
Lateral line
Caudal Peduncle
Caudal fin

BRILL

Scientific name: Scophthalmus rhombus

A close relative to the Turbot, this flatfish can be found in the same sort of habitat.

Coloration of this fish is a mottled grey and brown and can be practically transparent around the edges of its body and fins.

The skin of the fish is covered with thousands of minute scales. The Brill feed on small crustaceans and small fish.

Minimum size limit 14" or 35cm and although this species can grow in excess of 19lbs the united kingdom shore caught record is a little over 7lbs 6ounces.

DAB

Scientific name: Limanda limanda

previously known as Pleuronecetes limanda

The Dab is one of the smallest flatfish caught in British waters, although this species can grow in excess of 18" and over 3lbs in weight.

The Dab has a semicircular curve above the pectoral fin and the scales on the eyed side of the fish are rough when rubbed.

Colouration is a light brown to dark brown and in some cases speckled with a slightly darker colour.

United kingdom minimum size limit 8" or 20cm in length shore caught record stands at just over 2lbs 8 ounces.

DOVER SOLE

Scientific name: *Solea solea*

Also known as the common sole and black sole, this species of fish is found on sandy sea beds and tend to frequently turn up in sand eel nets.

coloration of this fish is a medium brown body with light and dark irregular spots, the under side is a creamy white. These fish tend to mainly feed at night, as a result most specimens are taken after dark.

Common sole is officially the correct name of this fish but the name dover sole has been adopted as this is where the fish was caught in large numbers and transported to London in the 1800's.

Minimum U.K. size limit 10" or 25cm with the united kingdom shore caught record just over 6lbs 6 ounces.

FLOUNDER
Scientific name: Platichthys flesus
previously known as Pleuronecetes flesus

Average size of this fish is around 1 - 3lbs, the body surface is rough particularly along the lateral line which is only slightly curved above the pectoral fin. Flounders usually have their eyes on the right side of the body, however in some areas about 20% of these fish have the eyes on the left.

Coloration of the Flounder is a light yellowy brown to dark brown, it is not uncommon to find orange spots on the top side of these fish, these are normally hybrids and should not be confused with the plaice. The underside of the fish tend to be like most other flatfish, a creamy white to pure white depending from where the fish has been taken as this can have a profound effect on the colouration, both top and bottom.

HALIBUT

Scientific name: Hippoglossus hippoglossus

The Halibut is the largest of all flat fish, with an average weight of about 25 - 30 lbs. (11 - 13½ kg), but they can grow to be as much as 431 lbs. (196 kg).

The Halibut is blackish-grey on the top side and off white on the under belly side.

When the Halibut is born the eyes are on both sides of its head, and it swims like a Salmon.

After about 6 months one eye will migrate to the other side of its head, making it look more like the flounder or Plaice.

This happens at the same time that the stationary eyed side begins to develop a blackish-grey pigment while the other side remains white.

Many anglers treat this fish in the same way as the Carp, going to extraordinary lengths to catch this species,
although the Halibut can be taken from the shore, most are caught around the northern reaches of the country and when you are lucky enough to land one they tend to be very small for this species.

All the larger fish are taken from the boat and not the shore.

There is supporting evidence that this species can grow in excess of 15 feet in length and over 750lbs in weight, however the minimum size limit is much, much lower at 22lbs or 10kg in weight, there is no minimum length on this fish as long as it is over the minimum weight.

There is no shore caught record set at the moment for this species, however the qualifying weight is set at 10lbs. If you intend to hunt for this species you will need to be prepared, there are records of anglers having one of these fish on the line for more than 4 hours and that's with specialist tackle and equipment from a large boat, if fishing for this species use a butt pad and very heavy tackle.

LEMMON SOLE

Scientific name: *Microstomus kitt*

The lemon sole is a right eyed flatfish with a small head and mouth.

The upper surface of the fish is reddish to light brown in colour but also mottled yellow and orange speckles with added yellow or green flecks, there is a prominent orange patch behind the pectoral fin.

The underside of the fish is white, Adult fish can reach up to 65cm in length and over 7lbs in weight.

This species is mainly caught from the boat and is quite rare from the shore.

Minimum size limit in the united kingdom is 10" or 25cm with the shore caught record of just over 2lbs 6 ounces.

MEGRIM

Scientific name: Lepidorhombus whiffiagonis

This species of flat fish is an uncommon visitor to the Southwest of the united kingdom.

The coloration of this fish is a light brown with lighter patches over its body, however at times this fishes body almost seems transparent.

The scales of this fish are quite rough and are easily removed so care should be taken when handling this species especially if it is being returned to the water.

Minimum size in the united kingdom is 10" or 25cm, although this species can grow to 4lbs in weight the average is more in the 2lbs range with the united kingdom shore caught record standing at just over 2lbs 5 ounces.

PLAICE

Scientific name: Pleuronecetes platessa

Similar in appearance to Flounder, the plaice only has bony knobs running from the eyes and over the head, between 4 to 7 in all.

The body of the Plaice is smooth with small scales, coloration is light brown with reddish orange spots.

Average size around the united kingdoms waters is up to around 2.5lbs however, this fish can grow in excess of 24" and 10lbs in weight, although this is very uncommon.

Minimum size in the united kingdom is 11" or 28cm and the shore caught record is just over 8lbs 4 ounces.

YELLOW SOLE

Scientific name: *Buglossidium luteum*

Also known as the Solenette, the Yellow Sole live on sandy or chalky sea beds, these fish tend to move in to shallow water during the summer months.

Coloration is a mottled light brownish orange and dark brown, there is a large dark spot in the centre of each pectoral fin, although the fin itself is extremely small.

This species can change its colouration to suit the habitat that it is swimming in, due to this the colouration can greatly differ from fish to fish.

There is no minimum size on this species at the moment, nor is there a united kingdom shore caught record, however this species can grow to around 6 inches in length and 4 ounces in weight.

COMMON TOPKNOT

Scientific name: Zeugopterus punctatus

The common topknot is a small flatfish that lives exclusively in rocky and broken ground, unlike the muddy and sandy ground that most flatfish prefer. As it is a slow moving fish it relies on camouflage to hide from predators, this small flatty is what is known as a left handed species and is almost round in shape, colouration is a mottled brown and white colour with light wide fins all the way round its body, this species has a very small tail. Average size is between 16cm and 22cm and the united kingdoms shore caught record stands at just over 12 ounces 6 drams, minimum size limit in the united kingdom is 8" or 20cm.

TURBOT

Scientific name: Scophthalmus maximus

Also know as: Psetta maxima

With the exception of the Halibut this is the largest flatfish caught around and off the United Kingdoms Coastline, this fish swims on its right side and the body is studded with small bony knobs.

The body of the fish is almost circular and a very dark brownish colour. The Turbot can grow in excess of 100cm although the average size caught around the united
kingdom is around 40 - 50cm, and average 2 to 6lbs in weight. U.K. minimum size is 16" or 41cm, shore caught record just over 28lbs 7 ounces.

RIGS TRACES & KNOTS

The main rule for making rigs or traces is that you use the same strength line for the main body as you have shockleader. For safety reasons this rule is printed below.

$\Rightarrow$ ***1oz lead = 10lbs strength line.***

$\Rightarrow$ ***2oz lead = 20lbs strength line.***

$\Rightarrow$ ***3oz lead = 30lbs strength line.***

$\Rightarrow$ ***4oz lead = 40lbs strength line.***

There are a few items that you will need to build the rigs in this book, they are as follows:

* A spool of shockleader up to 60lbs

* An assortment of floats complete with weights.

* An assortment of hooks, sizes 2 - 6/0.

* beads large and small.

* Assortment of swivels, rolling + barrel, sizes 8 - 4.

* Bait shields or clips.

* Snap links, purchased complete with swivels.

* Crimps, these help to cut down the tying of knots.

* Material for making stop knots, e.g. power gum.

* Line for making hook lengths.

* Zip sliders or other booms.

* Lead lifts for rough ground fishing.

If you have followed this list then you should have enough materials to make the rigs, or variations of the same in this book.

The art to making a good rig is to be able to tie a good knot and to tie the correct knot in the correct place, the use of crimps will work well on the right line, however if these are put on to tightly they can cut through the line, so although these may cut down on the tying of knots, these are not always practical.

The type of lead used with a rig is also very important, if you are fishing for flat fish it is best to use a dumpy lead as this will roll around the bottom and cover more ground, fishing a storm beach with a lot of current it is best to use a grip lead, this will hold the bottom and save the bait and weight from being washed onto the shore.

When fishing rock marks or places with a rocky bottom, the best weight to use is a plain lead possibly with a lead lift, this will help to retrieve the end tackle from rough ground. If the rig being used is for long distance fishing ,use a bait shield, this will help keep the bait intact during the cast.

SHOCKLEADER KNOT

Tie a half hitch in the shock leader, now push the end of the main line through the loop and pull slightly up. Now make a five loop UNI knot and using a little spit pull the two knots together and trim the ends.

UNI KNOT:

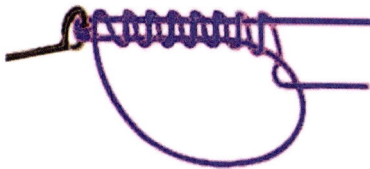

Push line through hook or swivel eye, pull 5 - 7 inches line through and make a loop, wrap through the loop 4 - 6 times. Now pull the line tight and trim end.

TUCKED HALF BLOOD KNOT

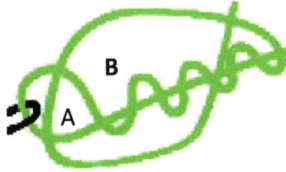

Push the line through the hook loop, wrap around 4 - 6 times, push end of line through loop "A" and then loop "B", pull up tight and trim the end.

CLINCH KNOT

Push line through hook loop twice, wrap line around it's self 3 - 4 times, push back through first two loops, now pull up tight and trim ends.

The above and previous knots with the exception of the shockleader are used for attaching the hooks and swivels needed for making end tackle, when using these always use a bit of spit when pulling them up tight, a dry knot is nowhere as strong as a wet one, pulling up a dry knot can and usually will damage the line and cause a weak spot that will ultimately end in the lose of end tackle or a fish.

Stop Knot

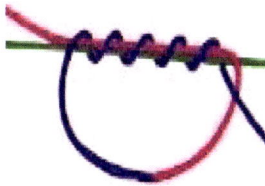

The stop knot is not used to attach anything to the line such as a hook or swivel. It is however used basically as a stop for the float and foremost to set the depth that your bait will settle.

This can be made from 15lb line, however there is a material made for this purpose called power gum.

To tie this knot firstly set up your rod and reel with a float system, take a rough measurement of between eight and twelve feet from the point of the hook and that is where you need to tie the knot.

First of all lay about eight inches of the power gum down the shockleader, then whilst holding one end about an inch in, take the other end and take it back towards the end being held so that you have a loop, now wrap the power gum around the shockleader and one side of the loop, you must do this at least four times but as many as eight, you must however wrap it around an even amount of times otherwise the knot will come undone. Once this has been done moisten the knot and pull up tight, trim the ends and now this knot should be able to be adjusted up or down the line but will hold firm enough to fix the float depth.

BRAIDED KNOT

This knot is normally only used by people plug fishing or from the boat where there is no great importance of casting and great distance, this line if cast is notorious for getting a birds nest, i.e. a bunch of twisted knots in the line.

Unless you are uptiding or downtiding there really is no reason to cast this line and when you do have reason, cast gently. firstly thread the main line through the eyes up the rod and then follow the diagram below, but pass the braided line through the swivel twice. When finished trim the end of the line but leave about a 5 mm tag, you should end up with something similar to the picture opposite.

Shore fishing Rigs & Traces

The following rigs and traces need a certain amount of materials to build them, a supply of the following will be necessary, beads, swivels, lead links, zip sliders, rotor clips, bait shields, and hooks from size 2/0 to 6/0, these can all be purchased from sea angling stores or in bulk online. A simple rig/trace making board is a very good idea, an explanation of how to make one follows.

DIY Rig/Trace Making Board:

A rig / Trace making board can be one of the best things that you ever manufacture and can be an indispensible piece of kit enabling you to make rigs and traces of all lengths and types.

One of the easiest ways to make this is to first find an old plank of pine, like an old floor or skirting board approximately   36 inches in length and around 4 inches wide, the reason for pine or similar types of wood is that the pins used in this board are not fixed and can be moved between the holes, these will pull out and wear in chipboard etc.

Any way you have your board, now all you need is an electric or hand drill with a 2mm wood drill bit, drill a hole about 10mm deep at one end of the board about 25mm from the end and approximately in the centre, now leave a gap of 150mm and drill a line of holes about 20mm apart and 10mm deep all the way to the other end. Now drill a further two rows as shown.

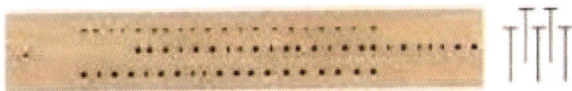

The pins used in this board are 2mm x 25mm round wire nails, this is the reason for the 2mm holes. When finished use a pin to secure a 3 way swivel in the top hole, work out the length of trace you require and fix a swivel of lead link using a pin in a hole down the other end of the board.

Making your first simple rig

After reading the first few pages you should have gained a basic knowledge of rigs and the components used, now follow this simple set of instructions and make your first rig, a single paternoster with a bait shield, note the bait shield is optional.

You will need the following parts:

⇒   *1, snap link, 1 lead link,*

⇒   *2 x swivels, 1x 3 way swivel,*

⇒   *1 bait shield optional, 1 x bead,*

⇒   *1 x crimp,2 x 18" shockleader material,*

⇒   *1 x 14" hook length material, 1 x hook.*

First of all connect the snap & lead links one to each swivel, now tie the free end of each swivel using a clinch knot to the 2 lengths of shockleader material, you should now have 2 swivels with links attached to the 2 shockleader lengths.

Attach the 3 way swivel to the free end of the shockleader on the swivel with the snap link.

Now feed the free end of the other shockleader through the rubber tubing and bait shield if used, make sure that the shield is the correct way up i.e. the cone is facing the lead link end, now slide on the bead followed by the crimp and let it run freely down the line DO NOT squash the crimp at this time, tie the free end of the shock leader to the other side of the 3 way swivel.

It should now look like the picture on the below.

If you are using a trace making board stretch out the trace between two pins so that it is taught, this will make it easier to set the hook length.

All you should have left at this point is the hook and the hook length material, now attach the two with a clinch knot and then making sure that the hook length is now shorter than the distance between the 3 way swivel and the lead link, attach the length to the 3 way swivel.

If used push the rubber tubing up on to the bottom of the bait shield, put the hook in place so that the hook length is taught, let the bead slide down to the top of the shield and then squash the crimp up behind the bead.

There you have it your first rig and remember practice makes perfect, a good thing to remember at this point is that most of the flatfish varieties tend to be attracted to brightly coloured beads, take this into account when attaching the hook length.

Anti-tangle spinning rig

One of the more popular methods of fishing for flatfish is spinning either with a baited spinner , spoon or just bait, to make the spinning rig you will require the following parts.

⇒ **2 x barrel swivels.**

⇒ **4 x beads.**

⇒ **2 x silicon tubing 10mm length.**

⇒ **1 x barrel lead.**

⇒ **1 x 1/0 to 2/0 Aberdeen hook.**

⇒ **1x 24 inch shockleader material.**

⇒ **Up to 12 brightly coloured beads.**

⇒ **1x 18 inch hook length, preferably clear.**

Tie a swivel to one end of the shockleader then thread the following, 1 x bead, 1 x silicon, 1 x bead, 1 x barrel lead, 1 x bead, 1 x silicon, 1 x bead and then tie the remaining swivel to the free end.

you should now tie the hook length to one of the swivels followed by the brightly coloured beads and then hook, the main rig body should look like the one below and you should have a anti shock anti tangle spinning rig.

Although beads can be used on all the flatfish rigs, these are not mandatory if the fish are in the area you are fishing you just stand a better chance of catching the species sought if you use an attractant like bright beads.

FLATFISH SNOOD

This beaded snood can be used on many different rigs, just by clipping it in place on the main rig body, directly to a swivel. The main use is for Plaice, Dab, Turbot and Flounder.

PARTS LIST

⇒   **1 Snap Link. 1 Crimp. 4-12 Assorted Beads.**

⇒   **12-24" Of Hook Length. 1 Hook, Size 1-2/0.**

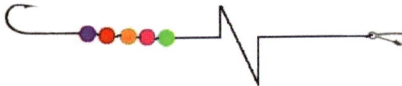

RUNNING LEDGER

This rig can be very versatile, catching most species of fish, particularly good for flatfish. This rig is made on the shockleader, this gives the fish a long length of line to run with, before the lead strikes out of the bottom.

PARTS LIST

⇒   **1 Zip Slider, with clip. 2 Beads.**

⇒   **1 Medium Swivel.**

⇒   **1 Hook, Various sizes to suit.**

⇒   **1 x 24 inches of Hook Length.**

With the exception of a few flatfish many of them are attracted to bright colours, this rig is a prime example of one that can be adapted, to do this just simply run a number of bright coloured beads up the hook length with either a small crimp or stop knot to hold them in place.

This works very well in cloudy waters.

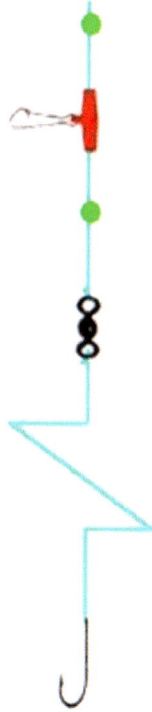

Pulley Rig

This rig can be made at any length as long as you are still able to cast it, however, the shorter the hook length on this rig the better it will work over rough ground, also this is the ideal rig to use if you are using a rod rest as this rig tends to hook the fish for you, however this does take out part of the fun and sport. This rig can also be fitted with the pennel hook system, this is made by threading a smaller hook up the hook length and then tying a larger one to the end, now twist the line around the shaft of the smaller hook finishing by pushing the larger hook through the end of the twisted line almost like a half hitch and then slide the smaller hook down.

PARTS LIST

⇒ **14-30" Of Shockleader. 3 x Beads.**

⇒ **3 x Medium Swivels. 1 x Bait shield.**

⇒ **1 x Hook, Size 2/0-6/0. 1 x Snap link**

⇒ **12-18" Hook Length.**

UP & OVER FLOUNDER RIG

This rig is ideal for putting a long flowing baited hook length on the sea bed the hook length has a number of brightly coloured beads on it, these act as an attractant and the hook size is quite small as flounder have relatively small mouths compared to most other species.

In this case the longer the rig/trace body the better the hook length will move around in the tidal flow.

It is good practice to either use a rig making board or a nail fixed in the wall to hang the rig body whilst fitting the hook length, if the later is used attach a weight to the end of the body, it will make things a little easier.

There are many parts used for making this rig, and every piece has an important role, these are listed over the page.

Making this rig to the correct specs will mean that it can be cast correctly.

PARTS LIST

UP & OVER FLOUNDER RIG

⇒ 24 to 48" Shockleader material.

⇒ 48 to 96" Hook length material.

⇒ 1 x Size 1 to 2/0 hook.

⇒ 1 x Bait clip & tube.

⇒ 1 x Bait shield & tube.

⇒ 1 x Swivel.

⇒ 1 x Three way swivel.

⇒ 2 x Lead clips/links.

⇒ Stop knot material, above bait shield bead.

⇒ Up to 12 Beads, various colours.

⇒ Note a crimp may be used instead of a stop knot.

⇒ Remember the brighter the beads the better they will work, try a few glow beads mixed in, they work very well.

FLATFISH SPOON AND RIG

A variation of a normal flatfish rig, this set up can be used in slight currents and can also be retrieved slowly to help attract the fish. It is always best to remember, to use smaller hooks for flatfish.

PARTS LIST

⇒   **1 Snap Link.**

⇒   **1 Small swivel.**

⇒   **1 Flatfish Spoon.**

⇒   **1 Three Way Swivel.**

⇒   **1 Weight Clip.**

⇒   **12-24" Of Shockleader**

⇒   **10-18" Of Light Hook Length.**

⇒   **1 hook size 1—2/0**

⇒   **2 x Split Rings, these may be needed, if not supplied with spoon.**

FLATTY RIG SINGLE

This flounder rig is very similar to the paternoster single with just a few modifications, first the bait shield and then the multi coloured beads on the hook length.

This rig is perfect for winter flounder fishing in estuaries around the united kingdom, but there is still room for improvement, simply by attaching to the lead end of the flounder twin via the lead link you have a triple hooked trace, however this is only possible if you follow the construction of the twin to the letter and use bait clips on the twin.

This rig will catch, with the right bait, all the members of the flatfish family with the exception of the halibut as a fish of this size needs a much larger bait , hook and trace.

The parts list for this rig is shown on the following page.

PARTS LIST

FLATTY RIG SINGLE

⇒ 24" of shockleader material.

⇒ 12 to 18" Hook length material.

⇒ 1 x size 1 to 2/0 BLN or Aberdeen hook.

⇒ 1 x Three way swivel.

⇒ 1 x Standard swivel.

⇒ 1 x lead link/clip.

⇒ 1 x Bait shield, tube and small bead.

⇒ Up to 12 various colour beads.

⇒ Stop knot material. Used for a stop on the hook length to keep the beads in place.

⇒ 1 crimp used above the bait shield, remember to set the hook length before crimping the crimp up tight.

⇒ Note a crimp may be used in place of stop knot.

TWIN FLATTY RIG

Again this rig resembles the paternoster twin, but with a few modifications, if you intend to use this rig in conjunction with the flounder single you must use bait clips as a shield used on this rig will upset the casting balance and may cause a tangle of hook lengths.

If however you intend to use this rig on it's own it is best to use a bait shield for the lower hook length on the main rig body.

When making this rig as with any other you must use the appropriate shockleader material to suit the lead being used, in the case of estuary fishing it is better to go up one level as you may find yourself using a heavier weight just to hold the rig to the bottom. Note: this rig when attached to the single can be hard to cast and will also pick up much more weed from the rising or falling tide in an estuary.

42

PARTS LIST

TWIN FLATTY RIG

⇒   **36" of appropriate shockleader material.**

⇒   **2 x 12 to 14" Hook length material.**

⇒   **2 x size 1 to 2/0 BLN or Aberdeen hooks.**

⇒   **2 x Three way swivels.**

⇒   **1 x Standard swivel.**

⇒   **1 x Lead clip/link.**

⇒   **2 x Bait clips and tube.**

⇒   **1 x Bait shield and tubing if using as a standard twin flatty rig set up.**

⇒   **1 x small bead, for bait shield if used.**

⇒   **1 x crimp if bait shield is used.**

⇒   **Up to 24 various coloured beads.**

As with most rigs a lead link can be connected to the top of this rig for quick change should it be needed.

ATTRACTOR RIG & SONAR TYPE ATTRACTOR

These rigs can be purchased as one part, sometimes without the hook length. These rigs are ideal for spinning worm baits across the bottom, mainly in estuaries. Mainly used for Flounder, these rigs will catch other flatfish, with slight alterations to the hook and lengths.

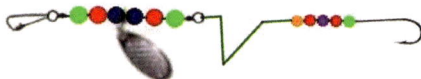

PARTS LIST

⇒   1 Snap Link. 1 Crimp. 3-9 Beads. 1 Attractor Rig. 18" Of Light Hook Length. 1 Hook, Size 1-2/0.

PARTS LIST

⇒   1 Snap Link. 3 Crimps. 6-10 Beads.

⇒   1 Sonar Attractor. 18" of Light Hook Length.

⇒   1 Flatfish Hook, Size 1-2/0.

INLINE FLOUNDER SPOON

Purchased in one piece, these Flounder spoons will work with most flat fish, if the right bait is used. It is often better to change the hook length and hook, these are normally short and the hooks can be blunt, in changing the hook length it is also possible to place coloured beads on this rig to act as an extra attractor.

PARTS LIST

⇒   **1 Flounder Spoon. 12-18" Of Light Hook Length. 1 Crimp. 3-12 Coloured Beads. 1 x 1-2/0 hook.**

The above spoon is one of many that can be purchased from angling centres around the United Kingdom, these come in a variety of shapes, patterns and weights. Spoons are best used for spinning, whether its for flatfish, Mackerel or even Bass, spoons used correctly can be deadly for a number of species, as stated above the diagram it is better to remove any hook already attached and substitute it with a hook length and replacement hook.

This method also works very well from the boat, however substitute the hook length for a 6 to 12" wire trace line, if making this up yourself you will need small crimps to secure the spoon and hook length.

BAIT & PRESENTATION

Virtually all of the fish sought by sea anglers feed on other forms of marine animal life, many of which can be collected by the angler around the mark that is being fished. The baits listed in this part of the book are the main baits used to catch the wide variety of flatfish, however these baits also have a habit of attracting other species such as Bass Cod etc.

The art of successful angling is to get the bait in its natural form into the area where the fish are feeding however, casting the bait out and keeping it in that state will depend on the type of end tackle or rig being used by the angler, it can be a waist spending all that time baiting up your hook or hooks just for it or them to get tangled in the main body of the trace or rig and end up scattering the bait over a wider area, this defeats the object of the exercise and bites tend to be fewer and far between.

The type of hook used can also influence the end

result and this is overlooked by many anglers, for instance the use of a worm type bait holder hook sounds great and in principle can work very well, however what no one ever tells you is that these also can cause the angler to use more bait, the main reason for this is that if they are not used properly, these tend to rip the insides of the worm causing it to loose it's juices quicker and get washed out, for this reason and this one alone most of the baits in this chapter are all put on fine wire Aberdeen or BLN's, these are simple to use in conjunction with bait needles etc. giving you well presented bait for all types of sea angling.

Crab Baits

In order for a crab to grow, it periodically sheds it's old outer shell, before this happens the crab develops a new soft shell under it's hard one, when this happens the crab takes in an excess of water which makes the soft shell swell, at this time the hard outer shell splits and comes off, leaving the crab with a soft skin which hardens off over a period of a few days to a week.

After a crab has peeled and the shell has hardened off, it will, if female, develop eggs, these are held by the crab under it's tail, these are normally orange to brown in colour. Crabs with eggs should not be taken, but should be returned to the water or under the rock from whence it came. Crab baits can be one of the most deadliest baits available for a variety of fish, Flatfish, Bass, Cod, Ray, Wrasse, and Rockling, are the more popular.

Crabs in their natural state can be used, if small enough, however these mainly work with certain species like Wrasse and Rays. Crabs that have recently lost their hard shell are known as soft backed, these are a very good bait for Bass , Ray and Wrasse if used whole with a hook through the back, from side to side, and the legs tied up the line and around the hook with bait elastic. There are a variety of different crabs that can be used for bait, most of these can be found on the shore line around the low water mark.

If you are collecting crabs yourself be sure to replace any rocks or sea weed that may be disturbed, this will give cover for crabs to return.

Preparation of a Peeler Crab.

Many anglers use this bait, however not all know how to prepare them. The following method is one of many and is a very basic one.The first thing to do is, to find or purchase your Peeler Crab, this can be frozen or live, however if you are going to peel this yourself, live Crabs are better than frozen, as many shops freeze these whole, without removing the lungs first.

If purchasing frozen peeler, check to see if the lungs are black, as these will deteriorate even when frozen.

The first stage of the operation is to remove the legs

and claws, this is done by pulling the leg at the socket, these are removed very easily. Do not discard the legs as these can also be peeled and used for tipping off the bait, or for cocktails.

Now remove the under shell, sides , tail and jaw bone, to do this , hold the crab upside down and with the nail of a finger prise up the shell and remove, this normally breaks in to many pieces. with your nail

pull up on the jaw of the crab, the bone comes out quite easily, now peel the tail by running your thumb nail down the centre of the tail and applying a little pressure, this wil remove the shell from the tail. The sides of the crab, by this time are falling off, remove these. With the crab in this stage, pull back the under sides and expose the lungs, these are like thin light brown fingers, behind these is a thin bone the size of the lungs, this must be removed. To do this use your nail and just prise the bone out complete with the lungs.

The final stage is to remove the outer shell of the body, this can be done at the start, however having the main shell still attached, will help to keep the main body in one piece. The outer shell should come off very easily as all the parts holding it have now all been removed.

Before putting this bait on to the hook, the best thing to do is to wash it, this removes any broken shell that still remains on the peeled Crab.

It is always best to obtain and use bait in it's fresh state, even live in some instances, however, properly frozen and prepared baits are always a good substitute.

Consideration for others and the environment should be uppermost when digging or gathering live baits, in many of the harbours and estuaries it is forbidden to dig bait in and around boat moorings as this can be dangerous to others.

Peeler Crab

Peeler crabs are shore crab and other varieties that have reached the point that their shell is too small and so this transformation is a part of the cycle of the crabs life, most peelers can be found by taking a closer look at the rear of the shell, just before they start to peel a thick light line appears along the bottom edge of the top shell, this eventually gets wider until it splits and the shell starts to rise up from the newly forming shell underneath. At this time in their cycle they are very vulnerable, at this time they also tend to pair up with either a male or female depending on what sex they are, they do this to mate.

Peeler crab is an excellent bait for many of the flatfish

51

varieties but if you don't collect it yourself, it can be very expensive. When using these for most species they need to be peeled, this is done by removing all of the shell from the body and legs, including the internal lungs etc. tis can be seen in the previous section on peeling a crab.

Any remaining sharp pieces of shell or internal bone will result in the fish spitting the bait out. don't waste the legs, pull the shell off and put them on the bottom of the hook.

The best way to present this bait is to once peeled place it against the hook and lightly tie it on with bait elastic making sure that you do not squeeze the juices out.

Worm baits

Lugworm

Lugworm is an excellent all round sea bait, it can be collected by the angler from estuaries and certain beaches, but care must be taken in doing so, many of the areas that these are found can be very hazardous and extremely dangerous, sinking sands and very sticky deep mud are just a few of the things that face the bait collector on a regular basis. If you are not sure about digging worms yourself, then it's better to leave it to someone that does it on a daily basis, these can be found in most sea angling shops and are normally quite reasonable, these work very well in certain areas for flatfish.

If collecting this bait yourself, store in a seed tray type container between layers of dry news paper in a cool place, preferably a fridge if possible, and never dig around boat moorings, this could cause problems for boat owners and bait diggers alike.

To use this bait, either use a bait needle or just thread the worm on to and up the hook, bring the point out just before the base of the worms tail, this is normally filled with a sandy material in fresh worms and will break off if you try pushing the hook all the way round, use up to two worms per bait.

Ragworm

Ragworm is another all round great sea bait with three varieties all working very well for flatfish, either on their own or mixed as a cocktail bait, these can be used singularly as in the case of the king rag or bunched in the case of the smaller harbour rag or in the case of the white ragworm which you will have to be collected yourself, used singularly on the end of a baited king ragworm bait just as a tip, these also work very well on their own on a very small hook for the smaller members of flatfish variety. King rag can be found on a semi mud and shale foreshore in many estuaries and some beaches, the harbour rag tend to be found in and around harbours, but also up muddy estuaries, the white ragworm however, is found mainly in coral type sand and in many cases around lugworm casts, these are highly prized and a fantastic bait to use.

Left to right: king rag, white rag and harbour ragworm.

When using ragworm be advised that they do have small pincers at the mouth end, if they do bite you it really is not that bad, in fact you wouldn't normally feel it, just seeing it is enough to know. The best way to hook theses is to wipe your finger across the worms mouth and when the jaws open feed it the hook in the same way you would a lugworm.

Sandeel

Sandeel are not a bait widely associated with many flatfish, but many anglers have the knowledge and don't always share it, Turbot, Halibut, dab and even Flounder feed on Sandeel when the fancy takes them, which in the case of young adults is when ever they can catch them, when you have your own favourite flatty mark and you know the fish are there try a small Sandeel fished very close to the sandy bottom, it will catch flatty's. So the small favourite bait for most species just happens to be a rather good bait for many flatfish.

You hook it the same way you would hook a worm, i.e. feed the hook through the mouth and gently feed the Sandeel up the hook, bringing the point out of the body about 1 inch from the tail, it is best to use defrosted or fresh eels for this, but now the bad point, it is such a good bait for all other species that sometimes you have difficulty getting through these species to reach the flatfish.

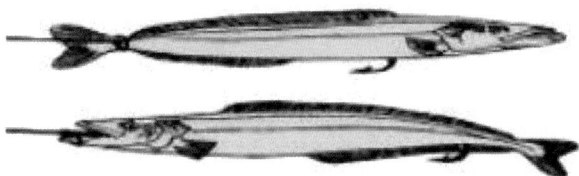

Note hooking a live Sandeel using the above method will kill it and defeat the object of using live eels which can be hooked by using the following method.

First of all you should hook live Sandeel in a way that the eel stays alive, hooking it in the tail and then dragging it backwards through the water will still catch fish but the action a live gives will be lost within the first few yards of the retrieve, for this reason live

Sandeel are best hooked through the back of the head as seen previously or by carefully passing the hook point through the open mouth out through the gap at the rear of the gill cover and the push the point through the very bottom of the eels body just past but below the fin.

Angling Methods

Estuary Fishing

Fishing an estuary is just like a mixture of rock and beach angling, you can get the deep water and the shallow sandy or muddy bottom, you will find all sorts of snags and rocks etc. but then you will also find an abundance of marine Creatures that feature in the staple diet of most species of fish.

The tackle you will require for fishing this type of area is a bass type rod fixed or multiplier reel, a variety of different sized and types of lead, loads of bright coloured beads and an assortment of Aberdeen type hooks, bait holder hooks can be used but these can be unreliable.

Attractor spoons can also be used, however, the use of these will take a different method of fishing.

A seat box can be a good idea in this sort of area also a rod rest will be needed, you will require a place to put your rod whilst you set up. A good pair of waterproof boots, Wellingtons etc should be worn in this type of area, caution must be taken if walking across sand or muddy banks in any estuary, sinking sand is very common in these areas, also if you get your foot stuck in the mud it can be almost imposable to remove it.

As with any fishing it is best to see the ground that you will be fishing over at low tide, make a mental note of any small streams, gullies or hollows that are present in the estuary, these will show where the fish swim, feed and tend to hold in as the tide drops.

Different baits will be present in different areas of the estuary so if you find the ideal spot for fishing from try to use one of the natural baits that are already there, these can be gathered by yourself or purchased from the local tackle shop.

If digging for bait please be a where of any local restrictions, bait digging is forbidden in a lot of counties or in a lot of cases harbours, around slip ways and boat moorings.

The best way to set up the end tackle is to use either a running ledger, pulley rig or a single or twin flatty rig, with a beaded hook length, use this instead of the plane ones on the other rigs, the variation and colours that can be used are up to you. In cloudy water use bright and even luminous beads, these do help to attract the fish.

Fishing an estuary can be difficult at the best of times, one thing is that you can fish these areas at almost any stage of the tide, if the fish swim up the river they have to come back down as the tide turns, this means that although anglers have their preferred times to fish these areas the fish are constantly swimming up and down the estuary.

When you decide to fish your chosen spot first cast a lead out into the water and check which way the lead drifts, normally this will be seaward if the tide is going out and inland if it is coming in. if using a running ledger then the best weight to use is a grip or pyramid lead, when this anchors you can let line out allowing the baited trace to cover more ground.

Always cast against the tidal flow this will help the lead and bait settle or you will find the baited end tackle will get washed into the edge and you very rarely catch fish in this area. Set your rod up with baited trace and weight now cast it against the tidal flow, let the lead settle and either hold the rod or place it in the rod rest, in this case if there is a fast current it can be very tiring holding the rod so if you have a rest then use it.

The rod will get a substantial bend in it however, this can be down to weed and this will tend to hamper your fishing through various stages of the tide, a quick short shake of the rod tip will normally remove this.

If a Flatty picks up your bait you will first see a sharp rattle on the tip of the rod followed by a sharp pull as the lead, weed etc. breaks free from the bottom. Now you will need to strike this, even if you don't have a fish on and you will never know unless you do.

The difference between using a rest and standing holding the rod in your hand is, ok you may expel a bit more energy but when that unmistakable rattle hits the tip of the rod you know there's a fish biting so you strike and reel it in, this will almost certainly have weed around the shock leader knot and possibly the trace swivel, now if the fish needs to be pulled in against the tidal flow you are better off walking down stream as you are reeling in, this will make it easier on you and the fish.

Once the fish is on dry land, remove the hook, plaice the fish in a suitable container, re-bait the hook, cast out and start all over again.

Rock fishing

First of all you need to find a rock mark that not only has water all through the tidal flow but also has a sandy bottom, flatty's are rarely caught on ground that is covered in rock and weed, being flatfish does mean that they tend to settle on the sea bed, in that respect the cleaner the better and that is a bit of a contradiction when they love to settle on a muddy bottom, but there you go, that's flatfish for you.

The tackle required for the task in hand is either a very heavy Carp rod, a bass rod or light beach casting rod and which ever reel you have to accompany it, the mainline needs to be between 10 and 15lbs breaking strain and a shockleader should be used for safety purposes.

The best end tackle i.e. rig or trace to use is either the

pulley rig, running ledger or flatty rigs, but the main aim is to get the bait on the sea bed and not floating off the bottom.

Unlike estuary or beach fishing you will not be able to see the area you will be fishing as it should always be under at least 12 feet of water, so the best baits to use in these areas are worm and crab baits unless you are targeting Turbot, Dab etc. in which case you really want a Sandeel on your hook.

Should you be targeting Turbot, you will need to hold the rod, this variety of fish tend to ambush its prey so the best thing to do is cast your baited rig out to sea, let it settle and then every two or three minutes give the reel two or three turns so that the bait is constantly moving across the sea bed., hopefully the turbot will end up ambushing your bait, when this happens you will need to strike almost straight away.

If fishing for other members of the flatfish family from the rocks you are better off using worm baits and although peeler crab is an excellent flatty bait, using it from the rocks might be a slight mistake as you tend to get inundated with bites from other species. A flatfish bite is quite distinctive, normally you will get a very slight tug on the line followed be a quick succession of taps or rattles on the rod tip, obviously the finer the rod tip the stronger they will show up.

So you are on your rock mark and have just had a bite, the first thing you need to do is take hold of the rod and slowly reel in any slack line, this shouldn't be a problem as flatty's tend to settle on the bottom fairly quickly after a bite, once you have reeled in the slack, slowly pull the rod tip back towards you, you should now feel the weight of the fish on the line, lower the tip reel in the slack and strike, but remember you are not trying to rip the fishes head off so don't be too rough.

Reel your fish in hand line up the rocks if necessary, do not climb down to the water, and once your fish is on dry land remove the hook and either put the fish in a suitable container or return it to the sea, re-bait your hook and cast it seaward once again, as the chances are that the first fish you catch will not be flat.

Beach Fishing

This type of fishing, although similar to rock fishing has a number of differences, you can use the same rod and reel depending on the length of the rod, the longer the length the better, however, remember even a light Carp rod can become heavy and uncomfortable to hold for a period of time.

It can be a good idea to carry your tackle in a seat box and carry a rod rest, this can be invaluable on a beach.

You will need an assortment of leads, different sizes and types i.e. plain and grip depending on the tidal flow, you will also need a number of Aberdeen or BLN type hooks.

Before you start to fish the beach, try and see what you will be fishing over, this can be very productive and will result in a more successful fishing trip, it is a very good idea to make a rough sketch map of the beach, roughly making note of any sand bars, gullies, rocks or areas of pebbles or broken shell etc. such areas are where most bait can be naturally found by the fish and therefore will be the areas that the fish move to when the tide moves up the beach, also make a note of any worm casts etc.

If worm casts are present on the beach at low water, this is one of the main baits to use when you start fishing, however, if there is a lack of casts on the beach, don't despair worm baits will still work exceptionally well. There is a myth that its best to fish so many hours up and down the tide, this is only a myth and unless you have it on good authority from someone you know or a listed in detail venue then the only way to find out is to fish it from low tide up and back down, this may sound a bit drastic but that is the best way to do it.

It is said that the best thing to do is to cast out to the third breaker as that is where the fish are, however apart from the fact that most of the best fish are taken from the first 12 feet from the shore, the other thing is that you are always retreating up the beach and if you have done your homework you will know where the best place to cast is and so the third breaker theory is also a myth.

Before you start fishing attach a plain lead to the end of your shock leader and cast it straight out into the surf in front of you, tighten up your line and just watch it for a moment, observe the drift, if the lead swings around very quickly then you will require either a heavier or a grip lead, however plain leads allow the bait to move around covering a larger area and in doing so helping to find the fish, but again if you have done your homework you will know where to cast and you will want your lead to stay in that area and in this case use a light grip lead.

The best rigs to use in this area are the running ledger, flatty rigs and the pulley rig, if you happen to be on a deep shelving beach one of the best rigs to use is the up and over flounder rig, this will obviously catch other flatfish. Unless you know for a fact that Turbot, Dab etc. are in the area stick to worm baits and again although peeler crab will work in this area you will stand more chance of landing a bass with this bait and not the targeted flatfish.

At the edge of most surf beaches you can normally find a rock mark that looks out across the beach, these are usually good places to fish for this species, however, you will find that you will have to use grip leads otherwise the bait ultimately ends up on the beach and trying to retrieve the end tackle can be time consuming and costly. Fishing from the rocks, you also find that the fish tend to bite differently, this is not because they are feeding or hitting the bait in an unusual manor but more down to the depth of water and the lack of tidal run on the line.

Just remember when fishing from the rocks at the

edge of the beach, you cast across the surf and not out to sea. Before you start fishing set your rod rest up at the edge of the surf and remember that you will have to move it back up the beach as the tide rises. Set your rod up with baited rig put your desired lead on the end and the cast out to sea, you are not trying to break the casting distance record just between 30 and 50 yards should be ample, let the lead settle on the sea bed and then reel up the slack line and put the rod in the rest.

Most flatty bites follow a particular set pattern, a sharp tug on the rod tip and then a short succession of taps, however, the time to strike is after the tapping, only strike gently, you can pull the hook and bait out of the mouth quite easily, if you miss this stage just raise the rod tip slightly and if the fish is still there it will normally take off, this can be a problem as a lot of the time the fish will swim at a great pace towards the beach giving you a lot of slack line, in cases like this you must reel up the slack and gain control of the fish or you will loose it.

Once you are back in control the fish will start to fight and you will need to keep the line tight, larger fish tend to feel as if you are just pulling on a dead weight, where as smaller fish just don't want to give in and can give great sport.

Once the fish has been landed remove the hook, put the fish out of the way or return it to the sea, bait up your hook and cast it back out to sea, remembering to move the rod rest back up the beach.

Boat Angling

Trolling

To use this method you really do need fixed rod rests on the sides or rear of your boat, these can be purchased from some angling stores and many boat shops at a very reasonable price. Very few boat anglers use this method, which is a pity as this technique can be absolutely devastating, catching large numbers of Mackerel and numerous other species.

Although I have used this method with a carp rod I wouldn't recommend it as the boat will be moving and putting a great strain on it a heavier rod is required for this technique and in most cases a six to eight foot twelve pound class boat rod is ideal. You can troll using either rigs, spinners, spoons or baited spoons, it's not what you use but more the method of moving the spoons or bait around the water that counts, this method works very well in estuaries, inshore and offshore, but care must be taken in estuaries as there are always boat moorings etc. to manoeuvre around.

If you are using spoons for trolling then apart from the weight you need no other end tackle, however should you want to use either a spinner or bait it is best to use a anti-shock anti-tangle spinning rig, this will keep the spoon or baited spoon on or just off the bottom.

With the boat stationary or slowly drifting lower your rig or spoon over the back of the boat, when the lead hits the bottom reel it back up one or two turns of the reel, this should move your spoon or bait away from the bottom sufficiently enough to clear most snags and as the weight will rise as the boat starts to move this should be an adequate depth to fish at, as your boat moves over deeper water you can let line from the reel to compensate.

Now put the rod or rods in the rod rests and start to move the boat, you do not want to be moving around the surface like a bat out of hell four to five knots should be more than fast enough to start with, as the boat starts to move forwards the lead will start to lift until your line is roughly at a 45 degree angle to the boat, if it doesn't reach this angle speed up slightly, or above that angle slow the boat down, but in all cases remember you need your bait more or less on the bottom. If the bait is high in the water you will attract other species.

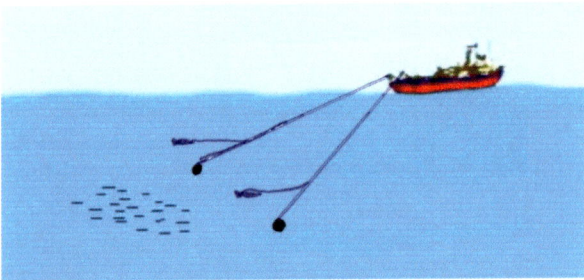

When a fish does take the bait you should take hold of the rod from the rest and reel in any slack line, this method normally hook the fish for you so there really is no need to strike and in doing so could lose you the fish, continue reeling in until you have the fish safely on the boat, remove the hook from the fishes mouth check all the knots and put it back in the water and start all over again.

This method can be very productive for Turbot over deep water sand bars using Sandeel for bait.

Deep Water Boat Angling

This part of the sport requires use of heavy boat tackle as the main species being sought is the Halibut, this fish can grow to well over 300kg however, the average size taken is more in the 11kg to 17kg plus range. Again as with all flatfish, the Halibut is found on clean sea beds the main problem is finding a charter boat that is actually going out hunting for this species.

The tackle required for this exercise is a 30lbs plus boat rod a heavy multiplier reel and heavy line preferably braid as this cuts down on drag etc in the water, you can get more of it on the reel and it also improves the bite detection.

End tackle starts off with having the correct weight, in this case you will require between a 12oz and 3 x 2lb boat weights, the line for the trace should be around the 60lbs to 120lbs breaking strain Dacron or similar and the swivels used should be around size 4.0, that is about the largest in it's class, the only other thing to get right is the hook size, these are huge compared to standard sized sea angling hooks and come in around the size 8.0, and should be the circle type, to give an example of the size, this hook will almost fill the palm of your hand.

71

The hook length material should be made of wire trace line of 60lbs plus, the main trace body can be made using Dacron or other braided material, however it is a good idea to make this in wire trace line also, the weight end of the trace should be made from wire. The parts required to make the trace are as follows:

⇒   **2 x 3 way swivels extra large.**

⇒   **1 x lead link, large.**

⇒   **2 x 8/0 Circle type hooks.**

⇒   **2 x 36inch 60lbs wire trace for hook lengths.**

⇒   **1 x 48inch 120lbs wire trace for main trace body.**

⇒   **1 x 36inch 120lbs wire trace for weight end.**

⇒   **8 x crimps for wire trace material.**

The trace shown over the page is what you should end up with when finished , please note this trace can be made from monofilament but it is not advised and as this species can grow over 650lbs you wouldn't really want to risk loosing such a prized specimen.

When using crimps try to use the correct tool, using pliers can over crimp and weaken the wire trace material, also note the top of the trace is connected to the mainline by a knot, use the braided knot at the front of the book for this.

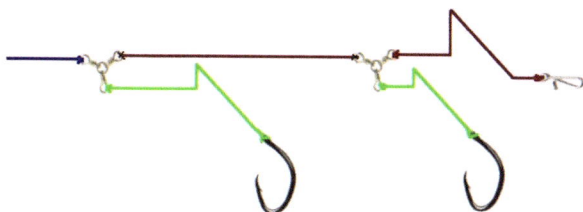

When you are ready to fish for this species lower your baited trace, the skipper of the boat will tell you the best bait to use and will normally provide it, over the side of the boat and make sure that the lead settles and holds the bottom, if not reel in and add weight, once this is done put the rod in a rest if one is available and then the waiting game begins.

Bites come as a sharp tug followed by numerous taps on the rod, unlike most flatfish, this one will normally run, if you have a but pad, now is the time to use it, put the butt of the rod in the place provided and start to take up the slack, at this time you will not know if you have an average fish or a monster, unfortunately you have to treat this as if it is the later.

When the fish is landed, maybe 30 to 60 minutes later you will know, this can be very hard work and not for the faint hearted.

Tight lines, have fun and above all be safe!

David

34479052R00042

Printed in Great Britain
by Amazon